HOW TO BE UNIQUE
(JUST LIKE EVERYBODY ELSE)

Sally,

Enjoy answering the only question that matters!

John Svoboda

First Edition
Printed in the United States of America

Book Design by Dane Davenport
Edited by Myra Svoboda and Dane Davenport

Cover Art by Dane Davenport
Front Cover Photography by Kelsey Brown,
kelseybrownphotography.com
Additional Cover Photography by Dane Davenport
Photograph of the Author by Jeff Burkhead/
Backstory Photography

Opening quote used with permission of Makenna Seghers

The events and stories in this book have been conveyed to the best of the author's ability, although some names and details have been changed for effect and to protect the privacy of individuals. Resemblance to any other persons, living or dead, events, or locales is entirely coincidental.

How to Be Unique, Just Like Everybody Else
ISBN 978-1-09838-537-8

Published by Svoboda Publishing
Lawrence, KS.
john@svobodaguitar.com

svobodaguitar.com
nobowtie.net

HOW TO BE UNIQUE
(JUST LIKE EVERYBODY ELSE)

Answering, "Why Am I Here?"
in an identity crisis world

JOHN SVOBODA

TABLE OF CONTENTS

How To Be Unique (Just Like Everybody Else)

Thoughts, and Guiding the Avalanche

Creating It, Creating You

TABLE OF CONTENTS (CONT.)

Essential Tools

Why You Are Here

"I'M HERE TO EXHALE THE BREATH OF
REALITY - IT WASHED AWAY IN THE
WATER AS I SWAM."

- MAKENNA SEGHERS

The Glimpse

Thumbing through the pages of a book something grabs you; an idea comes into focus like it has been chosen for you. Words click with meaning and you become compelled to investigate. As you read on, the wisdom in you is being pulled by the wisdom of the words; they speak directly to you. Understanding resonates within as ideas begin to flow with possibility. You feel a part of yourself come alive. You cannot ignore the buzz of possibility.

You have caught a *glimpse of your potential.*

If you have experienced the thrill of that sensation, then for a moment, you saw and felt the truth of what you are capable of achieving. The exciting result of your unique being; a proud accent to your individuality.

That *glimpse* first caught my attention for two reasons: First, because I know it is true. There is truth behind imagination, especially where emotions are involved. We cannot deny that a *burning desire* exists even if only in the recesses of our minds.

The second realization: the opposing reality. Knowing that I was spending the majority of my time procrastinating by giving attention to what I *should* be. I wasn't tilling the soil to let my uniqueness grow. Instead, I was working long hours at a model I was filling, rather than creating.

The *"glimpse"* is one of the greatest moments we can encounter. It is the opportunity to see that the door is open, waiting for us to step through.

Why Be Unique

We all know of people who stepped through the beckoning door and walked their own path. Often we define them as our heroes. On the other hand, we also know of people with talent, good health, and plenty of intelligence, who complain more than they create, burying themselves in what matters *least* while avoiding what matters *most*.

Potential yearns to be set free. When potential is defied and confined life becomes "hell on earth." But in the days (or even just moments) we choose to express it, we are enraptured in what can be described as "heaven on earth." And we all have potential for uniqueness.

So let's explore the base principles of becoming a unique expression of the self you desire, and conquering the only question that matters, from when you wake up, to when you put your head on the pillow - *"Why am I here?"*

The Wanderer's Intent

This book is for the wanderers, the seekers, and those who are already sharpening their edge. All can be elevated through awareness and specific action towards being more unique.

To those that *wander,* defined by indecision as much as decision, make no mistake, *inaction is a decision.* Lack of self-definition actively creates feelings of insignificance. And what we *don't do* to define ourselves can diminish the strength of our character. Absence is as life changing as the actions we *purposely* take. Unfortunately, we can become prone to procrastinating decisions, letting someone else decide, or not making needed decisions at all. Lack of proactive intent can grow as a *character trait.*

On the other hand, living with *specific* intent requires constant attention and decisions toward a preferred outcome. This "preferred outcome" is the pivot point at which uniqueness is both obtained and enjoyed.

Unknowingly, the *wanderer* also chooses outcomes. One denial at a time, a web is woven that obscures their individuality. If it goes on long enough, the web becomes a wall. That wall serves as the comfort boundary for all decision-making and keeps what is familiar as the decision base, overshadowing everything that is exciting and promotes growth.

I have the utmost sympathy for those pulled down by the multitude of life challenges such as physical conditions, family brain washings, a history of failures, and mental issues. However, everyone facing the question, "How do I define myself?" should reflect on if their answer is describing yesterday, *or tomorrow*.

Being *unique* is about taking what we have learned and shaping ourselves as we *move forward*.

George Burns described well the frame of mind I possessed when breaking through my own wall of denial: "I'd rather be a failure working on something I love than be a success at doing something I hate." I'll even take that quote one step further: I'd rather work towards my decided *intent* than be satisfied with denial.

Specific heartfelt intent is meaningful. It is nothing less than enlightenment to express:

I know who I am.
I know why I am here.
I know what I want.

I am unique.

The Unique Edge

Piercing through and grabbing another's attention takes concentrated efforts. The unique edge is what gives an advantage to those willing to own their style and work it into the world. It cuts through the spoils of disappointment and the bombardment of comparisons. It's how to carve out what will be, beyond what already was.

Everyone has unique qualities. It's similar to everyone having different tastes. But *innovative delivery* combined with style pushes ideas through the cracks.

The unique edge is what kept Steven Hawking carving away to his mass of contribution. It gave Helen Keller better vision than the resistance around her; discipline wasn't enough. From John Lennon to Leonardo da Vinci, the unique edge is what defined their existence.

*

Your Unique Voice

Does everyone really have a unique edge? Do you? Do you have the attractive "thing" that sets you apart and makes you enjoy what you offer?

There is an old fable of a journeyman, traveling alone with only one quest. Without this quest his life is not worth living and he has no personal worth to sustain his identity. After long miles of treacherous travel he encounters a canyon. Out of desperation he cries out for reason. From the echoing walls of the steep ridge he hears a sound. The sound gives him the comfort and confidence of his own existence. He is changed. He found his voice.

Finding the voice that is ours, and ours alone offers a connection in the world unlike any other. That I belong because I offer something worthwhile that pours from my truth, and in turn, *"Who I am"* manifests.

Being unique is more than feeling important, more than feeling popular, more than just being different, it is *knowing our voice and expressing with it.* Uniqueness pertains to originality and the source from which it comes. Integrity drives the desire to express it in ways that influence a positive sense of self-worth. There is completeness in its motion and security in its stillness.

My uniqueness is an expression of my flow; my interests and ideas come together in the expression. When I look in the mirror, I know I can do amazing things with the person looking back at me. It is the source of my smile as something connects with my truth, *my voice.*

Everyone has a voice. So if you can find even a sliver of a unique edge, swing hard, cut deep, and sharpen regularly. You will, then, carve out your unique existence.

when the soul shines in the mind

less thoughts have more meaning.

Finding Resonance

Do you love resonance? When two or more things vibrate together. One entity causing another to accept its influence, in a sense, becoming one; *the joining of like energies.*

Music resonates through the air in waves, the vibrations giving people the itch to dance to its groove. Stories resonate in the minds and imaginations of their audience. Laughter after a joke that resonates with our past experiences. Love resonates when walls of vulnerability are treated with respect. When spent in a resonate frame of mind, a great day is had. Some call it *flow.*

Resonance results when the *self* is ignited. It acts as a sign pointing out *who you are* in no uncertain terms. We search for it in entertainment, friends, art, activities, and careers. It tells us something is right and that we can open the door to let it in.

There is a buzz within resonance that says it's okay to be ourselves. Something that is *already in us* vibrates with what is happening around us. From the beauty of nature to the words on a page, an existence seemingly separate from ourselves gives us that which is already ours. In that moment of understanding we are more than an individual. We are connected, resonance proves it to be undeniable.

All descriptions of joy are descriptions of resonance. It is a beautiful experience while this electricity runs through.

Pray with it. Play with it. Look into the eyes of people with it. Give with it. Work with it. Meditate on it.

Above all, create it.

The Holy Ground

I can talk for hours of the many people who have rocked my world because they put expression of their *self* before the popularity of image. My list includes musicians, teachers, painters, sculptors, inventors, freedom fighters, friends, parents, writers, athletes, neighbors, storeowners, and politicians. The list of these self-contained warriors is endless, all of which put their unique intent before the resulting image.

Now what about you? Who do you admire for influencing your *desire to be your best self*? Why? What, in their intent, grabbed you?

Their essence connects with yours. The common qualities reflect your private collection of identity. You share a common ground. Absorb that influence while walking upon that holy ground in your own shoes.

The **sure sign** that indicates **your dream** is worth pursuing **?**

That you have one

Your Life's Purpose

Alexander Graham Bell sacrificed immeasurably to complete his idea for transmitting sound via electronic wire with what we now call a "telephone." His motivation, through the long nights and repeated failures, came from his desire to solve another, more important challenge. *More* important, because it pertained to his personal cause; to create what Miller Reese Hutchinson, another inventor, finalized as the first hearing aid. So why did Bell give such sacrifice to his time, research, cost, and trial and error repetition? Because Bell's *wife* was going deaf.

Mabel Bell was his focus. She suffered the effects of scarlet fever and Bell's motivation was the belief it was possible to restore the loss.

With no compelling vision, creativity dies. But when personal purpose is added to the recipe, the results are predefined.

Think back on an event that took all of what you have. Why did you do it? Why did you wade through the discomforts, disagreements, tensions, and setbacks?

If you feel you have no reason for what you do, *create one.* If *you* don't, who will? When that segment is left blank, we generally succumb to the decisions of others, leading up to endless feelings of dissatisfaction and angst around an inner lack of importance.

When we believe we are *unique* and enjoy it as an energy source of its own, our purpose tends to float to the surface.

Define your life's purpose or it won't have one.

Thoughts, and Guiding the Avalanche

Camping and the
Teetering Moment

The previous night I was in a state of mesmeric bliss. I remember standing in silence, intrigued by the way the branches were filling with snow. Limbs sagged with the increasing weight of the sticky flakes piling on them. Trees bent to the ground and blocked all view of what was previously a trail. I had rarely seen anything so beautiful; the forest catching a snow storm in the trees. It was pushed to the edge of what it could naturally support, yet stayed peaceful. Yet there I sat, in a warm motel, questioning the whole experience.

This wasn't the first time I'd been wilderness camping in the winter, but this time was different. With the temperature at 30 degrees and high humidity, flakes were the size of half-dollars. The forecast called for 12 inches of snow; I was already looking at 14 inches and it was still falling like confetti.

At midnight, I wanted to widen the view; get out and see the sky. I grabbed my brightest flashlight and headed down the path to a clearing. Gazing across the fields I sat absorbing the beauty they offered while covered in a blanket of white. I reached a bluff's edge and the landscape revealed a surreal scene of beauty.

Hiking back through the snow I realized I could not distinguish the trail from the woods; the trees had bent from the weight of the snow; many having their tops arch and reach down to touch the ground. It became a bit chaotic with direction so blurred. It was one person's hell, but to me, it was beautiful; I could *feel* the wilderness.

The game changed when I heard a loud crash and found that a large branch, five inches in diameter, had fallen in the path of my next few steps.

Back at the campsite, not more than twenty feet from the tent, I saw a tree had cracked and left its upper half piled on the ground. My mind tried to stay with the inspiration of beauty but something pulled at my thoughts. The snow had stopped and had turned to freezing rain. The forest threatened to fall, and I was in it.

I came here as an act of endurance; to be part of the adverse surroundings *is* to be with beauty, separate yet joined with nature. My intent was to endure no matter the discomfort, so as to soak in the experience.

Another large branch fell. That's when I packed a box with bare essentials, headed for the road, and set out to find a safe alternative.

The next morning, I woke up and looked out the window of the cheap motel room. The snow had fallen thick, cars inched along the highway, and the sound of spinning tires filled the air. My thinking had changed. I could not believe anyone would *purposely* camp in this weather. I had to question my intent - and my sanity.

The pleasure of the "call of the wild" began to fade. I saw the cold and wet as nothing but a nuisance. I saw no reason to continue my original plan. In the heated room of the motel, my toes were warm, the bed soft, and unlike the campfire, the light shined evenly on the book I read.

I decided to respond to what seemed like a break in my sanity. While enjoying a hot shower I saw a new outcome to this trip; I would go back in the morning, rescue the camping gear, enjoy a cup of stove-top camp coffee, pack and get the hell out of there. I saw no reason for staying.

Trekking through the snow and getting back to camp was difficult. What was previously an enjoyable challenge became work. My attitude flipped and my sense of comfort told me to leave. How it turned out I will never forget.

Looking at the shrunken tent, almost collapsing, from weight of snow and how branches the size of my forearm had randomly piled from the extra weight, forcing them to the ground, I made an agreement with myself: I would at least take the time to rationally reflect my plan for an exit. The packing would be tedious, yet comforting as I was heading out. And besides, it would allow me to get a cup of hot coffee in me to kick start the return.

Making the coffee calmed my attitude. Bringing the water to a boil hinted back towards the "I love camping" frame of mind. It was welcomed and delicious. Something about the smell of coffee in the cool air of the wilderness has always made me appreciate life. The heated cup warmed my fingers and drew my attention back to the stillness of the moment.

As I finished the coffee, the breeze brought in a chill that reminded me the temperature had fallen to twelve degrees; I needed to get warm. The kindling (that I wisely covered the previous day) allowed a fire to catch after I stirred the coals under the last surviving smoldering log.

The flames grew as I gathered more wood. The fire felt good; the air was crisp; and the fresh deer tracks reminded me of the pleasant solitude of camping.

As I saw beauty in the moment, ideas of staying would float to the surface. I forced my thoughts to stay on track with my intent: to *leave*. I recalled looking out the window at the motel and confirmed that decision again, without doubt, *leave*.

I took another sip of coffee and again noticed the fresh, easy to breathe cold air, the sounds of the quiet forest in the winter, and the smell of the campfire. Somehow, thoughts kept surfacing of wanting to stay.

At this point I struggled to understand the divide in my thoughts. If I thought of staying, I could also find thoughts and feelings to support it. When I thought of leaving, the same chain-link of support would appear. *The further I thought in one direction, the further I got from believing the other.* It was as if I was walking on a sphere. The further I travelled, the less I could even see the other side.

So, like anyone sitting on a frozen tree stump in the middle of the forest, with snow up to their knees (and half a cup of now lukewarm coffee), I decided to make a game of it; to play with my mind. Much like the snowball effect, the more I gathered thoughts in a chosen direction the more secure I felt about its truth. I could think it, feel it, and support it. I could turn it around and do the same thing in the other direction and find myself in a completely different reality. It became like a magic trick, **my thinking was forming my reality and I could create the reality I wished to experience.**

It was becoming clear. My thinking created my reality - not the other way around.

In every moment, our thinking is teetering on the brink of a full experience in the *chosen direction*. Choosing means acting from the *mind* first and the *experience* after that choice. In this simple example of my camping experience, it was *thoughts* of leaving and *thoughts* of staying that illuminated the power I had over the circumstance.

After deciding to stay, the clouds cleared, the temperature fell to almost zero, and I had a blast.

Change Your Thoughts, Change Your Life

This practice is not about positive thinking (even though it is a likely result). I am reminded, every day, that I can alleviate doubt, anxiety, tension, and depression by rewriting the little "thought stamps" I create. I selectively choose thoughts that can cause a good ripple effect; thoughts I can believe and give me a buzz to proceed.

I take about 45 minutes every morning with this (literally) mind-bending process. With pen and paper in hand I take note of my thoughts and change them for the better. Writing it down helps me to hold myself responsible for making the thoughts real. This sets the tone for possibility, gives me mental stamina to conquer roadblocks, and forms solid ground off which to push.

A friend from childhood went down an unfortunate path leading to addiction. After he recovered from the last of five rehabs, he has since stayed out of the clinic, off the drugs, and fulfilled a creative life. On the phone, while we talked about some of the lessons he had learned, he threw out a sentence of great impact. One I saw as the answer to most of life's challenges. He simply said:

"I knew I had to change my way of *thinking* or I would never be happy again."

Such a simple concept. It's the most effective life change available; the most important sculpture we can shape: *our thoughts*. And the same holds for you. Do you take time to do it on purpose, with strong intent? Or do you just hope the autopilot produces favorable results?

Grab a pen and paper. Be intentional. *Change* thoughts to create a better tomorrow. Make it a habit, a routine, make it the most important activity of the day.

Nothing worth doing ever happens without intention.

Are you **thinking** this way because of your **feelings?**

or are you feeling this way
because of your thoughts?

The Question

When facing each day, we internally ask some rendition of the following question: *"What should I do?"* It is a good question to ask. It resonates with what we believe and provides a sense of security. But then what?

There are better questions; questions that pinpoint *you* as the architect of your thoughts and life. Because for the most part, we *do* create our present life; situations, income, social status, friends, enemies (if you have them), location, body weight, schedule, and happiness.

So instead, start with: "What do I think?" and then immediately challenge it with the more powerful question:

*"What is **best** to think?"*

The first question addresses the past. What we already think, is a sum total of every perception up until now. Past content is not worthless, but it is definitely *worth less* than what is possible *now*.

The second question, "What is best to think?", addresses the present. It addresses our *potential*. By answering *this* question, you respond according to who you are, just not who you have been. Which is tempting, the past requires less thought. It repeats itself. We only have to remember it. But the past is no longer real. The present is real. Ready to shape as you please.

So what do you want? It's a simple question that doesn't take monumental depth to answer: I want more money. I want a new car. I want youth, power, some peace and quiet, to be skinny, for that guy/girl to notice me, popularity, Christmas to come, Christmas to be over, no taxes, adventure, my teenager to stop smoking weed, escape, and let's not forget where we started - "I want more money."

Whatever is on your list, wad it up and throw it away. We come up with answers like this while we race through a day of doing things we don't want to do. If you had all of the frivolous, quick fix, "snap of the finger" cures come true, *then what?* What would you want once you had everything you wanted? What do you <u>really</u> *want?*

This is the better question; the question that rocks our psyche; makes us all a little uncomfortable, wakes up a desire for vision, and helps to define why we are here.

Every day, do what you really want that makes you glad you exist. Do the things that attract importance; a change, creation, involvement, accomplishment, or result that makes a difference for the future. So start by asking the question and then answer it.

*"What is **best** to think?"*

Thought Sculpting

U pon completion of Michelangelo's statue of David, the sculptor was asked how he perfected his masterpiece, his response: "I simply take away everything that isn't." Just as Michelangelo sculpted marble into beauty, we can sculpt thoughts into unique and exciting lives. And we start by taking away what *isn't*.

For effective Thought Sculpting we *refer to the past only to use it for a better future;* lessons learned, anecdotes to summarize, metaphors that clear the path, and most of all, recognizing and throwing out the unneeded debris.

I pull from the past for ideas. Valuable thoughts are to be found here. Dig for these, but be ready to shift your weight forward again as soon as the jewel shines. This is not about nostalgia. This is about creation.

Sculpting the future means taking time to step away from the sculpture and remember why we started in the first place. By chipping away in the present, those thoughts will take a clearer shape. That's what the inspiration, hard days, and long nights have been about. This is the most enjoyable and powerful place you can be.

Something magical happens once you realize what you really want. Life gets simple. There are fewer complications and less wasted energy in a workday. Dark thoughts lift and are replaced by thinking that matters. Time, relationships, money, skills, ideas, and life in general are used in a more productive manner. Mountains become molehills and the gold nuggets are no longer sought, but forged.

Let the sculpting begin. You *can* create the future.

Listen to Your Soul

Do you want to hear your soul speak? Nothing reveals your uniqueness like hearing your soul. It resonates. It screams. It's fun.

Here are some simple directions to hearing your soul talk to you. Grab a piece of paper and at the top of a page write the following:

The most effective ways for me to achieve a great life, <u>despite the circumstance</u>.

Make a list. It can be a list of ten (a popular number for making lists) but if you come up with seven, that's great. If you find yourself flowing past twenty, even better. Regardless of the final number just let the list finish itself.

Under normal circumstance I can pound out what it means to live a great life. Most of it being clichés, and outcomes with simple decision making and little effort: "think abundantly, give more than I receive, follow the golden rule, plan for tomorrow." But a challenge comes when I add the words *"despite circumstance."* The list now becomes more potent, giving insight should my world be turned upside down, if a catastrophe hits, and if my mere existence is challenged. Ego is set aside and out comes a powerful view of an effective future.

This is *my* list:

1. Strengthen the body, exercise, and eat healthy (it's the only place where I live).
2. Think forward (let go of the image I am supposed to be and fill the image of my highest vision).
3. Develop talents (regardless of how I compare to others).
4. Be purposely and positively enthusiastic (spread what is good).
5. Forgive others and myself (stop poisoning my heart).
6. Use time each day to learn and declare what I want (nothing is more important).

7. Pay attention to who I am being (discerning who I am).

8. Follow my conscience (it's the closest thing I have to a relationship with God).

9. Address mental, emotional, and physical addiction (these always hold me back).

10. Regularly use time to observe nature (witness principles).

11. Do unto others as I want done onto myself (we are connected).

12. Allow vulnerability (the best teacher of my own growth).

After I made my list, I realized my soul had spoken.

I can exercise each of these principles under most any circumstance. This is my soul telling me that no matter what, short of actual demise, I can define and achieve a great life. I can *live who I am.*

Make your list, *despite the circumstances*, and move to a better place.

Anything **exercised** gains **strength**

Be specific.

Exercise Is The Problem,
Exercise Is The Solution

I won't suggest that you *start* exercising. *You already are,* and you may not see how it's *holding you back.*

Why do we exercise? In its positive light, it prepares us to better handle challenges that come. The race up the hill, the lift of the weight, and the exertion needed to stay on our game. It is a principle based fact: *Exercise causes strength.*

The most influential pivotal point of my life was realizing I am *always* exercising *something;* the good, the bad, and the indifferent. We are <u>all</u> exercising the habits and thoughts that *hold us back* as much as those that bring us closer to our wants and desires.

There is no such thing as lack of exercise - *it's all a matter of placement.* We are always getting better at what we repeat, even if we are getting better at what holds us back.

Exercise laziness and watch yourself get better at it. Exercise procrastination, and you will soon be an expert. That goes for overeating, denial, complacency, dishonesty, greed, cheating the system, being late, controlling others, passivity, false apologies, the list is endless! And *you will become stronger at each as you exercise them.*

It is possible, and unfortunately prevalent, to strengthen what we are *not.*

Strengthen your unique edge. Strengthen loving who you are. Strengthen positive vision. Strengthen what will make you proud tomorrow for what you did today. We tend to exercise according to how much we love tomorrow. Strengthen what is *best.*

Conscience, Be My Guide

For the sake of clarity we will differentiate between the brain, the mind, and the conscience.

The brain makes for a lousy guide. It is an organ designed for sensory input, cognition. Your brain does not differ between good and bad. A sunset and a car crash are the same opportunity: information to be processed. Having no *use* for feelings, the brain can easily bypass them in order to continue absorbing data. It is why we *scroll*, but it is not why we *care*.

The *mind*, on the other hand, is what gives *direction* to cognition. It guides the flood of information towards purpose. It is the organized motion of the activity that looks through your eyes. We don't "change our brains," we change *our minds.*

The conscience is the awareness that is woven through each of us. That it *feels right* to be kind, respectful, and compassionate. That we can make decisions based in discipline over pleasure. That we can respond to a "guilty conscience" with intent of resolve. That we can face rejection in the name of *what's right*.

The conscience is a collective yet subjective sense of individuality. It pertains to the whole, how to distinguish from it, yet contribute to it. It clarifies what is right and wrong; a distinction found in each of us.

Because this book is not about how to behave but how to be unique, I will not expand beyond the obvious ideology of the Golden Rule, but it is your conscience that will show you the best direction of who you are, why you are here, where you will find purpose and fulfillment, *and what you really want.*

The best days of my life were the days I acted on my conscience. My actions on those days made me feel good about myself, caused good experiences, and led to better situations in the future. On those days, *I lived and loved who I am.*

Want a
real
ADVENTURE
?

Follow your conscience

It's Not Easy

If all of this is true. If being guided by our conscience leads to lives we love. If sculpting our thoughts propel us towards happiness. If finding our voices gives us a sense of self-worth. If carving out a unique edge will define our impact. If the creation of resonance unleashes the flow of joy. If listening to our souls moves us to a better place. If living with specific intent leads to the fulfillment of our potential and the discovery of our unique purpose.

Why don't we work, every minute of each day, toward what we really want?

The answer: *It's easier not to.*

Raise your strength and use your mind to look past the ease of life and stay focused on the importance of living your one life to its fullest potential.

Yes, it's easier not to. We all know it.

So let's get to work.

Creating It, Creating You

Keeping Track of Who You Are

My house is littered with pens, pencils, and scrap paper with a promise that within every three feet I can exert the power of recording an idea. Sticky-note pads can be found in every glance around a room. The chalk board in the kitchen gets blanketed with more than just grocery lists. The voice-recording app on my phone has mental notes and musical tidbits from as far back as I've had it.

I record *intrigues, interests, ideas, inspirations,* and any *thought* that makes me vibrate with better energy than I previously had. They are *me*. I protect them and keep them safe; safe and ready to go. These recordings are flashes and chunks of who I am.

If you find your collection is filled with the words of works of others, do not be too concerned. I went through a phase of piecing together *where* I learned who I am. Most of the time, it came from outside of myself. This will likely be true for you as well. We all find resonance in the work, ideas, and uniqueness of others. Our aim now becomes knowing who we are *in reference to it.*

An oasis of self-knowledge can be found in taking time to reflect on the most prominent pivotal inspirations in your life; the ones that have impressed you despite life's challenges and the friction of peer influence.

Once a collection is assembled, put the pieces together, step back, *and remove whatever doesn't provide momentum.*

In addition to helping establish who you are, this process can also help you see who you are *not.* By comparing, and exploring your feelings, you can easily put experiences in one of two buckets labeled: *That's me!* and *That's not!* The latter of the two - throw away.

If you keep track of these connections, you will start to view the world differently. Self-definition will become flowing and easy. Decisions become effortless to make because you will have a solid reference of your being.

Keeping track of who you are in this way hits on the core inspirations that can't be ignored. The fantasy around it is just inspiration that keeps it afloat. Always seek the chunks of insight that you can do something about.

Assess who you are and simply let go of the rest.

Some people will try to control your thoughts

but not people who matter

Challenging Beliefs

The more deeply ingrained a belief system, the more we will defend that system. It's a defense that keeps us secure in yesterday's beliefs. But as we age, the hope is that we also grow.

One hang-up that's commonly front-loaded in childhood is that it's easier to sustain momentum of learned beliefs than to challenge them.

We were most often "trained" to think in ways that keep us included in the pack. Regardless of intent, that training shaped us from a young age. We learned lessons that profoundly affected our decisions in life - what success means; what happiness contains; how relationships should work; and what is worth pursuit and why.

Enjoying uniqueness means breaking free of paradigms that plague us and shape us. It's time to train and create ourselves as the person we want to be tomorrow.

Always question beliefs. Do they come from a place of conformity, rebellion, or of careful examination and self-reflection? Questioning the ideas that made you is the most important step toward combining who you are with who you want to be.

Examine your beliefs, the source of your beliefs, and the reason for keeping them. Examine your beliefs in comparison to your behaviors and see if you are honestly fulfilling the influence of what you are supposed to believe. If not, question it, reform it, and use it.

You can reshape beliefs. You can let go of the influence that holds you down and exercise the influence that creates *who you are.*

The Distraction Attraction

We can claim to dislike distraction, yet we are *trained* toward it. The world is constantly designed and redesigned to pull you farther into it. We are conditioned to enjoy it as if it is harmless. Being perceived as harmless is its best camouflage.

Society, technology, media, and even friends, train us to believe that the general occupation of our minds is what matters most; flip through a catalog, gossip, complain, watch reruns, and scroll, scroll, scroll. Whatever is needed to send our brains on autopilot over *distinct* creation.

Sure, it's fun to have games to play and mindless activities to fall back on, but as a way of life, our society has placed actual value on a plethora of activities that produce no beneficial result. It allows the control they desire. *They keep us shallow.*

The next time you find yourself scrolling beyond five seconds, stop, and ask the question, "What am I learning?" Distraction loves to offer the illusion of sweetness in what is *noticed*, not what is *important*. Distraction can become so compelling that we actually begin to believe it has worth. It seems so satisfying.

Addiction masks *self-definition.* Distraction hides it. Put the two together and it's the powerful formula to cause a lifetime spent on nothing of lasting value.

Answer the question, *"What do I really want?"* and you will still be challenged by the lure of meaningless satisfying activities. But now you can more easily detect the limit that defines "waste of time." You feel the pull of truth in a direct stream of energy. You will quit putting nickels in the slot machine of life and stop hoping to hear the bells say, "You win! You produced *nothing* but at least you didn't have to work!"

Never let the *distraction attraction* be the main motivation.

Ironically,
PROCRASTINATION
is one of the few things

that can't be
put off until tomorrow

Procrastination

Procrastination lures me back to the comfort zone that imprisons me. Temptation steps in, camouflaging itself as attractive rationalizations. Always repeating the same dialogue, "I'll do it, just not right now."

The sad truth is most of us constantly train procrastination to destroy all motion toward any kind of change that matters. Doing it *tomorrow* keeps us safe; it keeps things predictable. And besides, any rational person would rather have a pizza today and an exercise plan tomorrow.

Procrastination keeps us comfortable while we *don't* accomplish. Have you ever sat down to do the work and let the apps on your phone take precedence over flow of execution? It's the greatest characteristic of the amateur.

Procrastination and growth cancel each other out.

Comparison

We are swimming in a stream of comparison and the current is getting stronger. As technology rolls along, reaching anyone, everywhere, anytime, so does the development of comparison through social media. It measures not, "How am I unique?" but *"how do I compare?"* It formulates the façade of success and blocks the satisfying feeling of what is right for you.

Comparison is not all bad; it can motivate. Use it to learn what factors could play out in your personal expression. Enjoy extrapolating ideas that, in comparison, are better than yours and *benefit* from exploring them. The key difference lies in how it makes you feel. Feelings of completeness and expression must ride higher than those of inferiority or superiority. *Superiority is an illusion; uniqueness is real.*

Stay focused on your ideas. Develop your uniqueness. By doing one, you will cause the other.

Satisfaction

The best cooks in the world enjoy the finished product while tantalized by what they will create next; responding to what can be improved upon. They find meaning and purpose in the *journey*. Episodes of satisfaction are short lived in order to intensify the learning. The satisfied desire is a blockade to becoming unique. When we shoot for one, we exclude the other.

Long lines at fast food restaurants reek with the avoidance of feeling *complete,* but promise a satisfying soak in feeling *content.* Likewise, we can fill our time with junk habits that are satisfying in the worst ways. We must never give up meaning and purpose for the illusion of security and satisfaction.

We are here *to cut through repetitiveness with a unique edge.* Ask, "What does this lead to?" Does it move us *forward?* Does it strengthen or merely satisfy?

Cut the repetitive crap. Enough junk already.

Do not **decide**
IF
you should
move toward it

move toward it, then decide
IF
you should have

The Motivation Myth

The absence of motivation is one of the greatest creators of doubt, almost making it synonymous. The truth is you will find motivation and you will lose motivation. Understanding this cycle (and knowing how to work it) is a main player in enjoying and developing a unique edge.

Losing energy and momentum is part of the process. However there is one, and only one, solution that works: get back to work. Working toward an idea is what produces the kindling for restarting the fire that set the idea into motion in the first place. Do whatever is needed to *stay* in motion towards the desired intent.

Whatever is helping you ride the wave of self-discovery, stay with it. In other words, be unmotivated but do it *anyway.*

I Don't Have the Time for Uniqueness

Yes . . . you do.

Yeah, but...

Have you had mental conversations about even the simplest ideas only to have them automatically met with "Yeah, but..." as the response? Perhaps it was just your own mind, or "self-talk." This is the seed of thought that allows a mud pit, or when turned around, becomes a garden of possibility.

Helen Keller created a series of schools while having a life history of being blind, deaf, and unable to verbally speak. Steven Hawking, as a quadriplegic, wrote mind expanding books that shifted entire paradigms of science. He also invented a way to transfer thoughts to words by moving a stick, connected to a computer, with his mouth. Ludwig van Beethoven wrote his last four symphonies with one very impaling obstacle - he was completely deaf! He also suffered severe depression, episodes of poverty, and what would be termed today as schizophrenia. His ninth symphony "Ode to Joy", became the most respected classical symphony ever.

What did the three have in common?

First, they are human beings and like us, they want a better life. They wanted their purpose to be noticed, their concerns to be respected, and their voice to be heard. They strove to meet basic needs and felt their "tomorrow" was worth pursuit.

Also, each has a situation or condition where the obstacle easily blocks the view. They could have so easily given up with the first "yeah, but…" that easily shoots down dreams and possibilities. Instead, they put "yeah but…" on the shelf and got to work.

We all do it. We are all creators. Therefore, we are all naturally challenged by doubt. It's part of the package. The more creative the opportunity, the more procrastination we can muster. The two present themselves as one.

But the difference between those who create with intent and those who quit, is how to deal with the "Yeah but…" moment. Remember, *the brain doesn't care what it feeds the mind.* It will believe and exercise any thought planted, especially if a challenge is involved.

"Yeah but…" has an antidote - refuse to listen to it. Change the subject, or disagree. Do whatever you need to do to put doubt on the shelf and create the space where the energy becomes pride.

Start. Get to work. Keep constructing an outcome. Create something to learn from, then improve it according to your ultimate intent.

LIKE A DRUG

DOUBT

CAN BECOME

ADDICTIVE

hangover included

The Mental Monster

It shows up ready to exaggerate itself unto our demise. It dilutes dreams and it loves to support itself through failure. It has free will to destroy our potential. It has a mind of its own and a past to protect. It runs like a virus once it is let loose. Our thinking is skewed by this one demonic influence more than any other. It's not a frame of mind, it is a *physical* part of our cognition. Doubt impacts every part of your life and doubt *kills*.

Our brains are programmed to recognize potential dangers and to proceed, or retreat, using *caution*. The challenge comes when Doubt sees its move and overactive caution grows into full self-sabotage. Doubt pierces it's claws into our minds and distorts our perception of reality.

Like a murder scene in a movie it keeps you awake at night. It's fake, but in the mind, it is very real.

Doubt acts as if it knows the future. And it will do anything to scare you into creating that future for it. As it highjacks our momentum it becomes easy to fall for its attractive lure: *protection.*

Doubt does offer protection. Protection from failure, commitment, involvement, and creation. It builds a wall around *everything we fear and everything we desire.* It starts a spiral of momentum that won't stop until it wins. It wins by keeping us in our place; keeping us from stepping out of the past and into what we can become.

Symptoms start as procrastination and can quickly turn to nausea, insomnia, job loss, dependency, and depression. Meanwhile, an array of unhealthy habits arise to become routine. The more attention we give doubt, the more power it exerts over our lives.

That's bad news. But there is hope.

The good news is that while doubt is extremely powerful, it isn't real. It has no substance. It's not a thing, a tool, or a weapon. It only has the power *we give it.*

It is in the shadow of this mental monster that we can gain advantage over it. Work through it, get past it, step over it. Do not engage, we must move forward in its shadow. By letting doubt make the decisions you are agreeing that the past is good enough. *It's not.*

If you are in pursuit of any realm of a better life, and your ideas are clear, your intent is pure, and you are, for even a moment inspired, take this advice:

Do it, then decide if you should have.

Renew positive vision as often as you are able. Refine it. Keep throwing away the thoughts that don't pertain to the final outcome.

Just don't look back.

Hidden Talents

Back when I was in high school we would half joke about Terry. He had some talent, but not enough to cause demand for his ability. No, Terry's knack was for getting his foot in the door. He was always average on the instruments he played but he played them well enough. The joke would be about how far he could take it, always taking it further than we expected.

Many years later while I was in the studio working on a friend's next release, I was reminded of Terry's real gift. Waiting for a mix to be finished, I checked my phone. The text read, "Terry just got off tour with Michael McDonald (Doobie Brothers) and he's playing rhythm guitar in the Bob Seger tour!" Come to find out Terry served as a guitar tech for national headliners, played keyboard for Cindi Lauper's tour and has a list of references that would make anyone proud.

Then there was Toni. Toni showed awkward ability on the guitar. She didn't practice, so her skill level rarely increased. Her visions were bigger than her potential as a player. But we would enjoy conversations about life and being true to art. We would discuss the joy of personal expression. She had a great desire to be in a band, a specific band. But still, she struggled with the motivation of practice. Toni quit lessons unexpectedly and thanked me for the conversations. We lost touch.

Six years later I finished the day and turned on my TV to help me mellow out. In hopes to hear some humor, I stopped on Conan O'Brien. After the commercials, a band was featured as the musical guest.

There she was - Toni. Standing on the stage, playing a simple part and filling in a dreamy background vocal. What's more is she is playing with the one group that she once only dreamed to play with.

We reconnected. Over a cup of coffee, I learned she had played all over the world. Multiple tours in Europe, Japan, Iceland, and countless shows up and down the east and west coasts of the United States. I asked how she had gotten this far.

Toni reached out and grabbed an empty coffee cup on the edge of the table. What she said was simple but it was important:

"Anyone of us could've picked this up. I'm the one who decided to."

While she had talent, it wasn't talent that got her in the door. It was knowing which doors to open, which doors to knock on, and intentionally answering the question *"What do I really want?"* Answering that question was her main device for achievement.

It takes *some* talent to achieve anything of great desire. But let's be careful how we define talent.

Both Toni and Terry had desire.
In a sense, *desire* stands out as their talent.
And it can be yours.

Essential
Tools

Tools

The word *tool* takes on a different meaning when referring to developing a unique life. The tools in the following section of the book, are not tools in the traditional sense as much as states of being. *Humor* for example is a concept, but it can be leveraged to attract, relieve, and excite. Also effective: *time, enthusiasm, collaboration, talent, faith, discipline, inspiration, vision, ideas, intrigue, curiosity, and attitude.*

The more these concepts are viewed as tangible items the more you can use them to leverage your uniqueness into being, and therefore, enjoying who you are. It leads to better use of our tangible tools (computer, pen and paper, cell phone, audio recorder).

The best part is you don't need to make a shopping list. You already have everything you need. Use them, and enjoy as your life becomes what you want it to be.

Mastery

is the result

of giving

our **best** effort

to find the easiest way

Curiosity

C uriosity put a man on the moon. Someone let the thought fly, "I wonder what would happen if…" The next thing you know Russia is beat out of the race.

Thomas Jefferson was curious to see if there was a westward passage across the land to the Pacific Ocean. Now I can sit in Kansas eating strawberries grown in California. Curiosity opens doors. Curiosity is the *easiest* way to put creative thoughts into motion.

What would it be like if I…
Has anyone tried it *this* way?
It's against the rules but does it work?
How did they come up with *that?*
What happens when I put these two together?

Effective curiosity is in knowing that ideas are everywhere, filling our lives like air. While curiosity cannot be forced, it can be invited, noticed, and nurtured. It is nutrition for uniqueness.

Inspiration

Nothing is better than the magic elixir of *inspiration.* Inspiration gives sustenance to our very existence. It is a bulls-eye on the dartboard of creation. It is the promise land. It is as good as it feels and it is why we are proud to be human. Make no mistake; inspiration *is bliss.*

When inspiration strikes, value it like the fountain of youth. *Refine your skills in order to deliver its message.* Be in shape. Be ready. The more prepared the receiver, the more flowing the inspiration.

But what about when inspiration fades, misdirects, or won't show up when most needed? What do we do when we pick up the pen, the instrument, the tools, the computer, the keys, the book, the gifts, or even the kids, and find something has changed? When an empty feeling we can't quite explain has taken over and threatens to disconnect us from this life-renewing energy. What then?

We all handle this excruciating mental black hole differently. The following are ways to combat and win:

1. ***Keep a record of intent:*** Write it down. Post it on the mirror. Display it with honor. This is the reason for the effort. The approach might change but the intent has strength beyond the moment.

2. ***Gratitude:*** Be thankful for the *idea* (beyond the inspiration). Gratitude strengthens the purpose behind the plan. Being grateful can also elongate inspiration. *Gratitude is inspiration we can control.*

3. ***Be consistent:*** Consistency addresses the rebirth of excitement. It means that you are *regularly* at it. Water under the bridge contains flow and that flow brings the treasured feeling of purpose. Consistency binds to effectiveness. Effectiveness opens the door for inspiration.

And last, but not least:

4. ***Do the work, then decide if you should have:*** Have something to show, even if only failure to discard.

Intrigue

The world is an *interest and intrigue* workshop. They function as magnets, pulling *who you are* from the world around you. Some things, *many* things, do interest you. It's about paying attention to knowing why - *that* is the flow of *intrigue*.

Don't let go of the search. What was interesting yesterday was there to lead you to what is intriguing today. Keep it going. You may not know how to achieve it. You may not even know if it's possible. Don't focus on the *how*, keep your sights set on the *what*.

I'm certain that if you walked into a store called "Life Options" you could point out what you *do not want*. Just stay focused on everything else.

You just began.

Imagination

Vision is important; maybe the most important factor as far as a *foundation* goes. Vision is piecing together a plan based on what we know, what has happened in the past, and what we can research. But *imagination*, is what turns your vision into memorable moments and magical creations. It is what leads us to new territory, a better way forward.

Imagination walks the tight rope. It can go amazingly well; it can go incredibly poorly. It can become extreme and therefore, so can the results. But as long as imagination has a positive push, something good will come of it.

I keep a list of almost all of my imaginative ideas, even the ideas that don't work. If it came from a positive burst it will offer itself as a building block somewhere else. And if it doesn't, I'll hang on to it anyway (maybe someone else can use it).

After imagination fills the playground with ideas, I wrap the favorites together, and get back to vision.

Vision has the steady momentum.
Imagination has the breakthroughs.

Vision says: "Here are possible outcomes."
Imagination says: "And here are some ideas that make it an *adventure.*"

Ideas

Ideas are in rampant supply and can be devalued because of their seemingly endless availability. *Don't take this miracle of life for granted.* Ideas are the best gift the mind can give and the only way to exercise uniqueness. Ideas connect intrigue with involvement, problem with solution, *want* with *have.* Nothing reliably resonates in your brain like the clarity of an idea. Invite them in.

Sometimes ideas flow but sometimes we must seek them out. When you come upon a void in creativity, use the following ways to break the vacuum.

Have faith that the idea is already forming.

Your mind is prone to creating ideas that benefit the future. The mind wants to enjoy ideas. It wants to solve. It wants to create what hasn't happened. Your mind is capable of the idea you need. Let faith bring it to surface. We've all left a challenge to rest, only to later,

119

unexpectedly, have a magic light bulb go on with the solution.

Know the idea has a *place*.

It has a receiving station somewhere, somehow. Even mistakes can be the catalyst toward an answer.

Describe, *in detail*, what the idea will fulfill.

Getting specific can easily evolve into an act of creation. Describe what the idea solves and what will *grow as a result*. Write it down.

Brainstorm with intent.

Create a flow of thoughts that are centered on the need. Leave it alone and be ready. It will come. When we are open, the best ideas seem to come from everywhere, as if they have a mind of their own. And ideas *do* have a mind of their own. They don't like to be forced as much as fed. They desire simplicity and flow.

Do it a lot. This is the most important part.

Ideas are the mind's favorite activity. Let it dance in the mysterious wonder that brings all good things to life.

Collaboration

There are many qualities that stem from creative effort, of them, *possessiveness* is one of the strongest. We want to *own* our work, our direction, and *our way*. We can began to avoid, or even hide from, what seems to be stifling outside opinions.

This is one of the greatest mistakes we can make.

Collaboration has almost *limitless power* for bringing a unique expression to its highest point. Getting another mind involved is scary - we have to let go of total creative control. But letting go is precisely where the magic happens. Collaboration doesn't restrict our creative flow, it allows it to flow through others to places beyond our immediate grasp. Finding resonance in unexplored perspectives and changes allow our ideas to reach their highest form. Often collaboration is the only way to fully unlock that which we truly seek - *expression*.

There are endless examples of unique accomplishments that relied heavily on the inspiration and input of others, and few (or none) that went entirely without. It's frequently the music producer, not the writer, who is responsible for the sound and success of an album (i.e. The Beatles, Michael Jackson, Dwight Yoakam, Bruce Springsteen, Pink Floyd, Madonna, Chicago, Metallica, Motown, and virtually every piece of music you've ever enjoyed). The song is the idea, the final sound is shaped in collaboration.

Just as you think your uniqueness is complete, unlock the door and prepare to accept some changes; invite them in with open arms. This moment of awareness is also your moment of growth.

If you still find the need to control, have the *self-control* to let go, to nurture collaborative energy.

Only then can you can reach higher.

Faith

Beautiful, unfettered faith. It may not cause or cure, but it does allow strength to be had and used. It's the choice to trust beyond our present thoughts that something good will come. It offers the bridge to change and patience while it happens.

Faith, itself, does not cause something to happen. But it helps those who have it to accept the unknown. Live with it, knowing that while it is intangible, it allows ideas to roost, ready to be used.

Have faith as you till the soil, knowing your uniqueness will be had and that it will be worth the effort.

Discipline

Discipline streamlines intent. With it, we can conduct our lives according to our inner voice. The results are astounding. It is how we can impress ourselves. *Discipline is the best tool on the shelf.*

No other tool sharpens your ability like discipline. No other tool delivers who you are, with refined clarity, as much as the use of this one power hitter. Of your entire arsenal, reach for this tool and watch the others *become more useful with less effort.* It is the source of good health, financial success, solid relationships, spiritual growth, reputation, and most of all, creative output.

It is the source of staying clear minded, on time, creative, and physically fit. Its effectiveness is vast. Examples of its benefits are too broad to cover but it is the secret to reaching <u>every</u> result we value.

We are shaped to see discipline as a *behavior*; a habit we develop. It is not. *Choice* is the habit. We have all made choices, based on sincere intent, that sit unfinished. Discipline is the "go ahead", putting in motion the follow-through of that choice. *The more we use it, the easier it is* and the more we understand it.

It doesn't matter if you have talent *if you don't use this tool.* To not use it leaves talent inoperable; it will fade without it. It will atrophy and die. At any given moment we all have more discipline - *available to us* - than talent.

You do not have to have *faith* to have discipline. It helps, but when faith lacks, discipline will pick up the pieces and return the momentum. It is always within your grasp and will only strengthen the faith you have.

When ideas and purpose are combined, discipline acts as volatile fuel that causes combustion. The explosion is your *true self* being realized. It is a beautiful thing to understand that it is *always in you*, waiting for you to use it and enjoy the results.

Use it and enjoy the results.

Attitude

Elissa, at age nine, would show up to her guitar lessons in everything from Groucho Marx glasses (yes, the ones with the attached mustache and nose) to a full Cinderella costume. At every lesson I would ask how she was doing. Without hesitation, from the depths of a realistic, electric buzz, Elissa would announce, "I'm *awesome!*"

She would say it with her whole being, with eyes bulging out as if she just won the lottery. Her Cinderella dress would shake as she would try to hold back her excitement. Her guitar would be gripped ready to play. She would tell me of her day, which, no matter what took place, was also *"awesome!"* This little girl, right before my eyes, was demonstrating that she knew her happiness was a choice.

How do you think those lessons went? Not how she *played* in the lesson (sometimes better than others), I'm asking about the experience. You already know every lesson with her was fun and full of creative excitement.

Something about enthusiasm sets us free and also defines us; especially *positive* enthusiasm. I've never seen anyone who doesn't look great with a genuine smile planted ear-to-ear. An enthusiastic smile radiates what is held in the heart; the energy runs free to become contagious.

Positive enthusiasm sets us free, welcoming the whole person; mind, body, and spirit. And when enthusiasm is genuine, it lets our soul flow; it lets our uniqueness be known. *It is the energy of what we want to be.*

> **"It's your attitude**
> **not your aptitude**
> **that determines your altitude."**

That is a beautiful quote. I don't know who said it first, and I don't really care. But I can tell you who demonstrates it: the people you respect; your heroes, mentors, and leaders. It speaks for itself. We know when our attitude has gone sour and we know when we need a better one. Like it or not, we know it.

Having a good attitude makes the difference in how much we enjoy all experiences that follow. Being able to identify and shape an attitude gives longevity to any endeavor. More importantly, attitude is the direction and source of flow for enjoying *uniqueness*. Connecting to the world with intent is heavily reliant on the attitudes we *choose*.

Enjoy this higher truth about attitude: At anytime, and in any situation, we can change it for the better. When we make this powerful choice our world comes into view. Obstacles become diluted. Focus magnifies.

Why is this phenomenon so thrilling? Because this enthusiasm *is you*. It is your connection with your source. It is the fire in your heart. It is you announcing *you*. Choosing an enthusiastic attitude is a liberation that is sacred to your being.

It is *awesome!*

To **change**
for the **better**

We have to **think** higher
than how we *feel*

Time

This is the only tool that will wear itself out whether you choose to use it or not.

Do that which is you, and do it *now*.

Why You Are Here

Finding Your Passion,
Whatever That Means

I have lost track of how many times someone has interrupted a conversation, concerning positive change, with a statement reflecting some rendition of: "It would be so much easier if I *knew* my passion."

What does that even mean? If you know what it means, you are likely aware of yours already and can continue without analyzing it. But continually wondering why you don't have one only *confirms* its absence.

If you seek *passion* follow *curiosity,* especially if it *inspires*. That is the seed of passion and can naturally grow into interest and *intrigue*. Intrigue soon sparks imagination and you begin work to bring *ideas* to life.

The more we do it, the more we experience who we are. And we refer to a person who regularly works their curiosity toward an end goal in an intentional way: "Passionate."

Don't **change**
change

Just be
awake

and know that you will

What It Takes

For those of us who struggle with thoughts of not having *what it takes*, this is your page.

<u>*You do.*</u>

Any time you caught a *glimpse* of your potential, you also caught a glimpse of the sum total of what it takes to express it. You saw that to *some* degree you are disciplined. You saw that, if even just a little, you are ambitious. You saw what you can *become*.

You have *some* motivation. You have *some* imagination. You have 24 hours a day - you have *some* time. You have *some* ideas. You have talent of *some* sort. You can discern perspective. You have *some* faith, attitude, and vision. *You have some of all it takes to be happy, successful, and unique.* And *that* is what it takes.

Using it? That's the chapter *you* will write.

Stay **focused**

It *will* happen.

And if it doesn't?

Stay focused. It will happen.

The Third Hour

When working on an idea, I like to bring the session to an end just after I've touched the other side, meaning I've worked new ideas into place as far as today requires. For me, it most often happens in the third hour; that's my pivot point. That's when the best ideas connect and form and flow.

It's as if time disappears, skills are stretched, and the chain-link of ideas finds conclusion to the vision and efforts. Don't misunderstand, many good things come in the spontaneity of the first hour; a rush of creative imagination finds its way through the stagnation of repetition. But the third hour allows me to work it and make the ideas solid.

The second hour gives room for challenging brainstorms. It allows breadth for speculation of the final outcome. But it's just not adequate time to challenge the quick-fix with the long-term vision.

But in that third hour, I can rework, reconsider, explore options, and most of all, become engrossed in the *result* I'm looking for. Simplicity becomes the rule and all senses support it. The littering of rambled thoughts subsides. The voice of doubt gets sucked down the hole from where it came. The ideas that I've been working are given space to tell their truth. Momentum pulls toward the center of reason. Inspiration goes from being *used* to being *reborn*.

Perhaps you have a different name for it or a different length of time? I know it as the *third hour*. When do you find that stretch that lets you know you gave this session all you've got? If you don't know, now is the perfect time to find out. Find the point you can hear your mind telling you, "That's all for today. You've done your best."

This is where you will find everything you've been hoping for. Welcome home.

To Be or Not To Be

My highest intent is to encourage you - and everyone - to take further steps in learning and engaging in what makes you, *you.* Getting out of the auto-thought that camouflages distraction, and begin to invent the beautiful uniqueness you know you can enjoy. Take it to the best *you* that can be imagined, and spread that new-found creation in hopes that other people become interested, intrigued, and have ideas of how to apply their inspirations to enjoy this wonderful state of mind.

We live in an identity crisis world. Media controls the vision of ourselves more than ever before. Perhaps this is not you or me, but we still interact as a whole and have constant influence on the mental health of people in our homes, villages, and communities.

I feel blessed to be able to share my insights and to possibly encourage a better tomorrow by respecting the conscience today. I believe it is a mental game. I also believe I have won that game, but I know the game is replayed every day and in every moment.

It is my greatest desire to influence you towards how truly and deeply happy you can be by developing your center; that part of you loves to be unique, standing unflappable in the uncertainty of life, knowing…

You are a light unto yourself.

B